Pangolins

Victoria Blakemore

Copyright info/picture credits

Cover, Janie Goodyer/Shutterstock; Page 3, 2630ben/Shutterstock; Page 5, SAP IBRAHIM/Shutterstock; Page 7, Janie Goodyer/Shutterstock; Page 9, Maciej Czekajewski/Adobestock; Pages 10-11, Iuliia Sokolovska/AdobeStock; Page 13, scubabiker/AdobeStock; Page 15, 2630ben/Shutterstock; Page 17, Foto Mous/Shutterstock; Page 19, 2630ben/Shutterstock; Page 21, Foto Mous/Shutterstock; Page 23; Kelsey Green/Shutterstock; Page 25, Andre Coetzer/Shutterstock; Page 27, Bobby Bradley/Shutterstock; Page 29, Maggie Meyer/Shutterstock; Page 31, Asmus Koefoed /Shutterstock; Page 33, 2630ben/Shutterstock

Table of Contents

What Are Pangolins?

Pangolins are mammals that have hard scales all over their body.

There are eight different kinds of pangolins. They differ in size, color, and where they live.

Pangolins are the only

mammals that have scales.

Size

Some kinds of pangolins are very small. They can weigh as little as 3.5 pounds and be about twelve inches long.

The giant ground pangolin can grow to be nearly six feet long and weigh over 70 pounds.

The giant ground pangolin

is the largest of the eight

pangolin species.

Physical Characteristics

Pangolins have long claws

that are good for climbing

and digging.

They have a long tail that

they can wrap around their

body. Some kinds of

pangolins use their tails to

hang from tree branches.

Their hard scales cover most

of their body.

Habitat

Pangolins can live in
rainforests, forests, swamps,
and grassy savannas.

They are usually found in
places with lots of insects,
such as ants and termites.

Range

Pangolins are found on two continents: Africa and Asia.

Habitat destruction is
becoming a problem for
pangolins that live in Asia.

Diet

Pangolins are **insectivores**, which means that they eat only insects. Their diet is made up of insects like ants and termites.

They are sometimes called "scaly anteaters."

Termite mounds like this are home to millions of termites.

Pangolins use their claws to dig into termite and ant hills, then catch the insects with their sticky tongue. Their tongue is very long can be up to sixteen inches in length.

Some pangolins break strips of bark off of trees to look for insects.

Communication

Researchers believe that pangolins use mainly scent to communicate with other pangolins.

They use scent markings to mark their **territory**.

Mother pangolins may also use sound and touch to communicate with their babies.

Movement

Pangolins that live in areas with lots of trees may use their claws to climb. They have also been known to swim.

Pangolins can run by standing on their back legs and using their tail to help them balance.

Pangolins are usually

slow-moving animals.

Pangolin scales are made from **keratin**. They are hard and have sharp edges.

If a **predator** is nearby, a pangolin will roll up into a tight ball. The predator can't get past the scales and usually leaves the pangolin alone.

Pangolins that are rolled up can stay safe from predators like lions, tigers, or leopards.

Pangolin Life

Pangolins are **solitary** animals, which means that they spend most of their time alone. They are very rarely seen together.

Some kinds of pangolins sleep in trees, others dig burrows under the ground.

22

Pangolins are mostly **nocturnal**.

They are active at night.

Pangolin Babies

Pangolins usually have one or two babies. Baby pangolins are born with soft scales that harden a few hours after they are born.

They spend the first few months of their lives riding on their mother's tail.

Pangolins are fully grown by the time they are about two years old.

Life Span

Not much is known about how long pangolins live in the wild. They are shy and tend to stay away from humans.

In **captivity**, pangolins have been known to live as long as twenty years.

However, pangolins are very

hard to keep and do not

usually survive in captivity.

Population

Pangolin populations have been getting smaller each year.

Four species of pangolins are listed as **vulnerable**, while the other four are **endangered**.

There are not many pangolins

left in the wild. It is thought that

they may be **extinct** soon.

Pangolins in Danger

Pangolins are often hunted by people for their meat, skin, and scales. Since they are so slow-moving, they are usually easy to catch.

More than one million pangolins have been traded **illegally**, more than any other animal in the world.

There are laws to protect

pangolins from being hunted

and traded.

Helping Pangolins

People are trying to educate others about pangolins.

They hope that if people know about pangolins and the problems pangolins face, they can help.

Glossary

Captivity: animals that are kept by humans, not in the wild

Endangered: at risk of becoming extinct

Extinct: no more left

Illegal: against the law

Insectivore: an animal that eats only insects

Keratin: the protein that makes up human nails and hair

Nocturnal: animals that are active at night and sleep during the day

Predator: an animal that hunts other animals

Solitary: living alone

Territory: an area of land that an animal claims as its own

Vulnerable: an animal that is likely to become endangered

About the Author

Victoria Blakemore is a first grade

teacher in Southwest Florida with a

passion for reading.

You can visit her at

www.elementaryexplorers.com

Also in This Series

Also in This Series